GARETH STEVENS
VITAL SCIENCE
Earth Science

PROPERTIES
OF WATER

by Alfred J. Smuskiewicz
Science curriculum consultant: Suzy Gazlay, M.A.,
science curriculum resource teacher

 Gareth Stevens
Publishing

A WEEKLY READER COMPANY

Please visit our web site at: www.garethstevens.com
For a free color catalog describing Gareth Stevens Publishing's
list of high-quality books and multimedia programs, call
1-800-542-2595 (USA) or 1-800-387-3178 (Canada).
Gareth Stevens Publishing's fax: (877) 542-2596

Library of Congress Cataloging-in-Publication Data

Smuskiewicz, Alfred J.
  Properties of water / Alfred J. Smuskiewicz.
    p. cm. — (Gareth Stevens vital science - earth science)
  Includes bibliographical references and index.
  ISBN-10: 0-8368-7764-0   ISBN-13: 978-0-8368-7764-9 (lib. bdg.)
  ISBN-10: 0-8368-7875-2   ISBN-13: 978-0-8368-7875-2 (softcover)
  1. Water—Juvenile literature.   2. Hydrology—Juvenile literature.   I. Title.
GB662.3.S63   2007
551.48—dc22   2006033113

This edition first published in 2007 by
Gareth Stevens Publishing
A Weekly Reader Company
1 Reader's Digest Rd.
Pleasantville, NY 10570-7000 USA

This edition copyright © 2007 by Gareth Stevens, Inc.

Produced by White-Thomson Publishing Ltd.
Editor: Walter Kossmann
Designer: Clare Nicholas
Photo researcher/commissioning editor: Stephen White-Thomson
Gareth Stevens editorial direction: Mark Sachner
Gareth Stevens editor: Leifa Butrick
Gareth Stevens art direction: Tammy West
Gareth Stevens production: Jessica Yanke and Robert Kraus

Science curriculum consultant: Tom Lough, Ph.D., Associate Professor of Science Education,
Murray State University, Murray, Kentucky

Illustrations by Peter Bull Art Studio
Photo credits: CORBIS, pp. 4 (© Karen Su), 11 (© Steve Wilkings), 14 (© Roger Garwood & Trish
Ainslie), 30 (© Roger Russmeyer), 38 (Chris Lisle), ©istock.com, pp. 5, 9, 10, 12, 16, 17 (both), 18 (both),
20 (both), 23, 24, cover and 25, 28, title page and 39 (both), 40; NASA, pp. 22, 34, 36; NHPA, p. 8.

Cover: Iguazu Falls in South America is part of a jungle ecosystem that is protected by Argentine
and Brazilian national parks on either side.
Title page: Constructed between 1931 and 1936, the Hoover Dam was the largest dam in the world
at the time.

Printed in the United States of America

2 3 4 5 6 7 8 9 10 10 09 08 07

TABLE OF CONTENTS

① INTRODUCTION

Where would we be without water? Water makes up most of your body. It makes up much of the food that you eat. It is in the atmosphere and in the ground. It fills lakes, oceans and seas, and riverbeds, and—in its frozen form—it creates glaciers, icebergs, and ice sheets.

A Special Substance

Water is special in many ways. It's the only substance that exists naturally on Earth in all three phases: gas (water vapor), liquid (water), and solid (ice). Unlike most other substances, it is less dense as a solid than as a liquid—the reason ice floats in a glass of soda and icebergs float in the sea. The way its molecules line up also gives water a high surface tension, which means that it can form into droplets of rain. Surface tension also allows certain animals, including water strider insects and basilisk lizards, to run across its surface.

Water is involved in all the weather changes that you experience. Some days, it rains or snows. On other days, the weather is dry. Water falling to the ground makes the grass, flowers, and trees grow. Sometimes, however, water also is part of severe storms, such as hurricanes, that cause enormous destruction and loss of life.

▼ A huge chunk of ice breaks off Viedma Glacier and falls into Lake Viedma, in far southwestern Argentina.

Water is responsible for many other changes on Earth. Over thousands and thousands of years, flowing water carves out deep, winding riverbeds, and melting glaciers leave deposits of clay, sand, and rocks that form into high ridges called moraines.

Essential for Life

All living things depend on water for survival. Some organisms, such as fish and whales, live in large bodies of water. Many other organisms, such as birds, snakes, and people, live on land but need to drink water or take in water with their food. Forests need water to grow. Even plants and animals living in the deserts depend on small amounts of water to exist.

Throughout history, people have built their farms and cities near sources of water. People have used water to grow crops, to drink, to operate factories, and to produce electrical power. Rivers and oceans have always been important for transportation, ranging from daily deliveries of cargo to historic voyages of exploration.

Today, scientists are searching for water in other places throughout the universe, including Mars and other planets. Because scientists believe that life on

▲ Rice grows in watery terraced fields in a form of irrigation used for centuries by farmers in Asia.

Earth began in water, the presence of water on other planets raises the possibility that life might exist elsewhere in space.

People today are also tackling a number of problems related to water. Water pollution and water shortages pose serious threats to this extremely important resource—threats to the survival of many species and to the economic well-being of many people.

So where would we be without water? We would be nowhere at all. In fact, we can thank water for everything we have.

2 WATER'S REMARKABLE PROPERTIES

Water is the most common substance on Earth as well as the most unique. No other substance can do all the things that water can do, because water has a number of properties that no other substance has.

The Water Molecule

A single drop of water contains millions and millions of molecules, the tiny particles that make up all forms of matter. Molecules are made of even tinier particles called atoms. A single water molecule is made of two kinds of atoms—two atoms of hydrogen combined with one atom of oxygen. This atomic arrangement gives water its well-known chemical compound name of H_2O.

The hydrogen and oxygen atoms in water molecules are held together in chemical bonds, the special kinds of bonds linking one atom to another. An atom consists of particles called protons and neutrons, both of which are found in a central part called the nucleus; an atom also consists of particles called electrons, which surround the nucleus. In a chemical bond, one atom shares its electrons with another atom.

Water Molecule

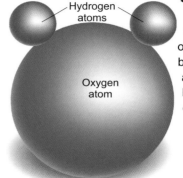

Hydrogen atoms

Oxygen atom

◀ A water molecule consists of two atoms of hydrogen bonded to one atom of oxygen by the sharing of electrons.

Water molecules are firmly linked to each other in another kind of bond, called a hydrogen bond. In this type of bond, the hydrogen atoms at one end of the water molecule have positive electrical charges, while the oxygen atom at the opposite end has a negative charge. The positive charge at the end of one molecule attracts the negative charge at the end of another molecule.

Water is the only substance on Earth that can be found naturally in all three

Other Hydrogen Bonds

Some hydrogen bonds involve attractions between hydrogen atoms and nitrogen or fluorine atoms, rather than oxygen atoms. In one of the most important processes of life, hydrogen bonds made of hydrogen and nitrogen are split between the two strands that make up deoxyribonucleic acid (DNA), the molecule that makes up genes. This splitting allows the two DNA strands to separate and then each act as a template, or model, for a new strand. Because of this process, when a cell of your body divides, each new cell gets a new, identical copy of DNA.

states of matter—gas, liquid, and solid—within normal temperature ranges.

As a gas, water takes the form of water vapor, for example like the steam that comes out of a heated teakettle's spout when the temperature has reached water's boiling point, 212°F (100°C). Water vapor is released into the air by puddles, ponds, lakes, oceans, and other bodies of water in a process called evaporation. The water molecules in vapor move about quickly, violently bumping into one another.

Besides mercury and ammonia, water is the only naturally occurring nonorganic (not made by biological processes) substance that exists as a liquid at normal temperatures on Earth. The molecules in liquid water are close together and move about freely.

When temperatures drop below water's freezing point, 32°F (0°C), water turns into a solid—ice. The water molecules in ice are far apart and almost motionless, locked together in six-sided crystals. Thus, unlike most substances, which contract as they get cooler, water expands after it cools past 39°F (4°C). This is why a given volume of ice weighs less than the same volume of liquid water; it is also the reason ice floats.

States of Water

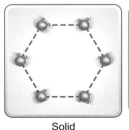

Solid   Liquid   Gas

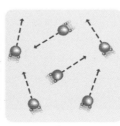

◀ In ice *(left)*, water molecules are firmly locked together in six-sided crystals and can barely move. In liquid water *(center)*, the molecules are linked but can move freely. In water vapor *(right)*, the molecules move about independently and rapidly.

Universal Solvent

Water is known as the "universal sol-vent," which means that almost any substance dissolves in water. This is important for many reasons. Bits of rock and soil dissolved in water move from place to place in rivers. Nutrients, nour-ishing substances, dissolved in water flow through plants and animals to nourish their cells. Molecules of oxygen dissolved in lakes and other bodies of water are breathed in by fish and other animals.

Surface Tension

Have you ever watched insects, such as water striders or whirligig beetles, walk-ing and skimming about on the surface of a pond? This insect capability is possi-ble because water molecules are locked tightly together. The force that causes the molecules of a substance to be attracted to one another is called cohesion.

These cohesive forces are especially strong among the molecules at the sur-face of a body of water, forming a thin,

▲ An Indonesian Lizard uses wide flaps on its hind feet to run across the surface film of water.

The Mosquito Life Cycle

The larvae of mosquitoes, called wrigglers, live in water. They look like small worms with wide heads. To breathe air, a wriggler pushes a tube at the rear of its body above the surface film of the water. After several days, a wriggler changes into a pupa, an inactive shell-like stage that hangs upside down from the water surface, getting air through tubes sticking above the surface. The adult mosquito develops inside the pupal shell in 2 to 4 days, after which it pulls out of the shell, dries off, and flies away. Most male mosquitoes live fewer than 10 days; females may live more than 30 days.

filmy layer at the top of everything from the sea surface to the edges of water droplets. Because surface tension results when water molecules cling together tightly, drops of water form tiny balls as they drip from a faucet.

Capillary Action

Surface tension is responsible for another unique property of water, called capillary action. This is the ability of water to climb up surfaces that it touches. Capillary action works because of strong attractive forces called adhesive forces. Adhesive forces act between molecules of two different kinds—such as the molecules that make up water and those that make up the sides of a drinking straw.

Capillary action helps water do many important things, including moving through soil and through the roots and stems of plants. It also helps blood, which is mostly water, circulate through your veins and arteries.

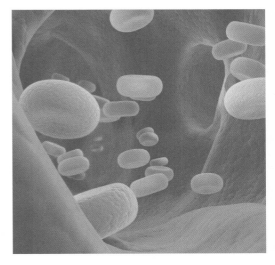

▲ Red blood cells flow through an artery. Blood is able to flow through veins and arteries because of capillary action.

Heat Capacity

Water has a greater heat capacity than any other substance—that is, when water is heated, it absorbs the energy from the heat, but water changes its temperature very slowly. Lakes, oceans, and other large bodies of water absorb heat from the Sun and release it much more slowly than does the land or air. Breezes blowing over these bodies of water carry warmth to the land in winter, thus moderating the weather of the area. For example, because of the moderating effect of Lake Michigan, during the winter the temperature in downtown Chicago, Illinois, is often a few degrees higher than the temperatures in Chicago's suburbs, except for those suburbs along the lakefront.

Evaporation and Condensation

Have you ever noticed that water disappears from a pan or bowl that's left out in a warm room? This happens because the warmth gives the water molecules more kinetic energy—in other words, the molecules move around faster. As the molecules speed around faster, chances increase that they will break free of the bonds that hold them to the water's surface. The escape of the molecules is what happens in evaporation.

Transpiration is a special type of evaporation in which water passes through the leaves of plants into the air. This helps regulate the plant's water balance.

Another type of water action you may have noticed happens when the bathroom mirror fogs up as you take a hot shower. This is called condensation. It occurs because the warm, moisture-filled air

cools when it touches the mirror's surface, which is cooler than the dew point, the point at which the air is saturated with, or full of, water. The cooler temperature causes the water vapor to condense into droplets of water on the mirror.

Condensation happens often in nature. For example, as moisture-filled air rises and cools in the upper atmosphere, the vapor condenses into droplets. These droplets of water make up the clouds in the sky. Other examples of condensation are fog, dew, and frost.

▲ Frost, a type of condensation, forms on the surfaces of plant leaves and a flower bud.

Power and Energy

Water can pack an enormous amount of power and energy. The force of water slowly and gradually shapes the land over thousands or millions of years through erosion, the wearing away of land. Falling

rain wears away mountains, flowing water in rivers carves deep canyons, and the pounding waves of oceans shape shores and cliffs.

Waves are disturbances in bodies of water that carry energy from place to place. A water wave, like a sound wave or a light wave, can be measured by its height, amplitude, wavelength, and frequency. Wave height is the vertical distance between a wave's crest (high point) and trough (low point). Amplitude is the distance from the wave's crest to its resting level, between the crest and trough.

▲ The crests of ocean waves rise above the wave troughs in spectacular turquoise arcs off the coast of Hawaii.

Wavelength is the distance between two crests or troughs that are next to each other. Frequency is the number of waves that pass a given point in a given amount of time.

Waves are set in motion mainly by the wind. The way they then move depends on various factors. One such factor is the amount of surface water over which the wind blows. Waves in the middle of the open ocean pass through the water

Seiches and Tsunamis

High winds, earthquakes, or changes in atmospheric pressure can cause long, high waves called seiches on lakes. In these kinds of waves, the water moves up and down but not forward. Some seiches can be more than 10 feet (3 meters) high. In the ocean, undersea earthquakes and landslides can cause waves called tsunamis. The waves, often less than 3 feet (1 m) high as they move across the open ocean, can develop into walls of water more than 100 feet (30 m) high when they crash onto the shore.

without moving the water forward. In shallow water close to shore, however, the wave crests crowd together, pile up, and cause the water itself to move forward.

Influences on Water Movement

The motion of waves and currents in the ocean and large lakes is influenced by many things, including some that are out of this world!

The gravity of the Moon and the Sun is responsible for the tides, the periodic rise and fall of ocean waters and other large bodies of water. Tides, which can be noticed best along ocean shorelines, are large bulges in the water resulting from the combination of the gravitational pull of the Moon and the Sun on Earth's water.

The heights of tides vary throughout the year. When the Moon and the Sun are in line with each other and Earth, the combination of gravity is strong, resulting in the highest kind of tide, called a spring tide. Spring tides happen twice a month, during the full moon and new moon. When the positions of the Moon, the Sun, and Earth form a right (90-degree) angle, the combination of gravity is weak, resulting in the lowest kind of tide, a neap tide. Neap tides happen twice a month, when the Moon is in its first- and third-quarter phases.

▼ Often debris marks where the last high tide occurred on a beach.

Wind currents are the driving force of ocean currents. Both are influenced by the Coriolis effect, which is the result of Earth spinning around on its axis. Because Earth spins around, any object that you think might follow a straight path over the surface, such as a cannonball shot out of a cannon, actually ends up following a curved path. This is because the planet is moving beneath the object.

As the path of the wind curves, it blows the surface currents of the ocean in curved paths. Because of the Coriolis effect, winds and currents in the Northern Hemisphere are pushed to the right of their direction of motion; winds and currents in the Southern Hemisphere are pushed to the left. A common misconception is that the Coriolis effect also makes water circle bathtub and sink drains in different directions in the Northern and Southern Hemispheres, but the Coriolis effect is actually not strong enough to influence such small bodies of water.

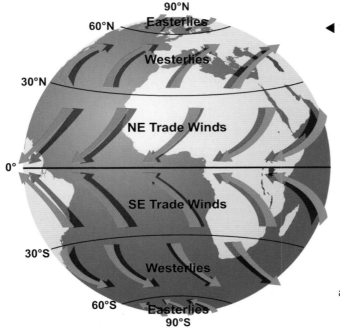

◀ The Coriolis effect causes winds in the Northern Hemisphere to swerve to the right of the direction of motion. So winds traveling south swerve toward the south-west. In the Southern Hemisphere, winds swerve toward the left in the direction of motion. So winds traveling south swerve toward the southeast. The arrows in this picture depict the movement of the winds. Ocean currents move some-what differently because they are affected by landmasses.

③ WATER'S IMPORTANCE

Why is water important? How many reasons can you think of? There are probably more reasons than you—or anyone else—can think of. Some of the many ways that water is important in the natural world are explored in this chapter.

Origin of Life

Chemical and geological evidence indicates that the first, simple, single-celled forms of life arose on Earth more than 3.5 billion years ago. These cells were similar to today's bacteria.

No one knows exactly how or where the first living cells developed. However, scientists have proposed a number of possibilities—all of which involve water.

According to one theory, molecules essential to life combined with each other in the atmosphere. Rain then carried

▼ Rock formations in Western Australia may have been created when microscopic organisms in the sea caused ocean sediments to adhere together in a variety of shapes more than 3.5 billion years ago. These formations may be the earliest fossil evidence of life.

these molecules down to the sea. Somehow out of this molecular soup, the first living cells came to be.

Researchers interested in the origin of life have tried to mimic the chemical and physical conditions of the early ocean in small experiments in the laboratory. Although no living things have been created in these experiments, scientists have succeeded in creating amino acids, complex molecules that are the building blocks of proteins which in turn are the building blocks of living tissue.

According to another theory, the first living cells arose in thin films of water on microscopic particles of clay. Amino acids or other complex molecules may have combined with each other in these watery films, resulting in living cells capable of making copies of themselves.

Animal and Plant Physiology

Every living thing is made mostly of water. Your body, for example, is approximately two-thirds (66 percent) water. A chicken is about 75 percent water, and a potato is about 80 percent water.

People are able to live without food for several weeks, but they will die within a week, if they do not drink water. The human body, as well as the bodies of other animals, uses water to carry out the

Percent of Organisms Made Up of Water

Organism	Percent Water
Tomato	95%
Earthworm	80%
Pineapple	80%
Corn (ear)	70%
Elephant	70%
Human	66%

many processes of metabolism—that is, the chemical processes by which cells produce the materials and energy needed for life. For example, the body uses molecules from food to produce complex proteins that build tissues.

More than half the content of the blood is plasma, a solution that is 90 percent water. Many chemical reactions take place in the plasma. It is in the plasma that nutrients, hormones, antibodies, and many other substances are dissolved. Once nutrients from food are dissolved in plasma, blood carries these essential substances to every tissue of the body through the circulatory system, the system of blood vessels that spreads like a vast network throughout the body. Veins and arteries are vessels of the circulatory system. The body uses nutrients for energy and growth.

Another extensive network of vessels, called the lymphatic system, carries lymph, a watery solution consisting of plasma, proteins, and white blood cells. White blood cells help the body fight infections caused by bacteria and other microbes.

Photosynthesis

Water is an essential ingredient that plants use to carry out photosynthesis, the process in which light energy from the Sun powers chemical reactions combining carbon dioxide with water to make carbohydrates. Carbohydrates, which include sugars and starch, are needed by plants for growth. Animals that eat the plants, or the animals that eat these animals, take in the carbohydrates and use them for energy. As a by-product of photosynthesis, plants release oxygen into the atmosphere.

Water moves through plants in vessels that are like the veins and arteries in the bodies of animals. There are two main types of water-transporting vessels in plants. Xylem vessels carry water from the roots to leaves and other parts of the plant. Phloem vessels carry carbohydrates from the leaves to the other plant parts.

▲ A cross section of the stem of a sunflower plant shows many vessels used to carry water and nutrients through the plant.

Water in Different Ecosystems

Water exists in very different amounts in different ecosystems, systems that are made up of living organisms and their relationships with their environment. There are small amounts of water in deserts and large amounts in rain forests. The plants and animals in each kind of ecosystem have special adaptations to allow them to survive in these different environments.

Deserts

Rainfall is scarce in deserts, where the loss of moisture through evaporation is typically greater than the gain of moisture through rain. Most deserts receive less than 10 inches (25 centimeters) of rain per year. In addition, temperatures in deserts often soar above 100°F (38°C) during the day. You may wonder how anything can live in these conditions.

Although deserts have fewer species, or biodiversity, than most other ecosystems, there are many species of plants and animals that have evolved adaptations to live in these harsh places. For example, most plants in deserts grow far apart from each other so that the roots of each plant have a better chance of getting at the small amounts of water that are available. Some plants have extremely long roots to tap deep supplies of water. The roots of the mesquite tree may reach as deep as 263 feet (81 m).

Some plants have special ways to store water for future use. The barrel cactus swells up while it takes in large amounts of water during the rare desert rains. The cactus gradually shrinks in size as it uses this water to live during the next long dry period.

Many animals living in the desert avoid the hottest, driest parts of the day by feeding only at dawn, at dusk, or during the night. Desert ground squirrels stay in a dormant, or inactive, state underground all summer to avoid the harshest period of heat and dryness. Certain desert toads lie dormant in the mud for much of the year until the rains in the spring coax them out.

▼ Organisms with special adaptations to live in the desert include the barrel cactus, which can absorb large amounts of water during rains; and the desert ground squirrel, which is active above ground only when it is relatively cool.

Rain Forests

You might think that organisms in tropical rain forests have it easy. In these woodlands of tall trees, which grow at or near the equator, it usually rains more than 80 inches (203 cm) per year. Rain forests are home to more than half of all plant and animal species.

However, the organisms of rain forests often have to deal with their own problems—namely too much rain. Heavy rains wash valuable nutrients out of the soil. Some rain-forest trees counter this problem by taking in the small amounts of nutrients found in rainwater that collects on their leaves or along their branches and trunks. Certain kinds of fungi grow in or on the roots of other trees, helping the roots absorb nutrients and minerals.

To shed excess rainwater that might weigh down and break their branches, some trees have leaves with grooves and drip tips, which pour water out like a pitcher. Other plants have leaves with oily coatings that help the leaves shed water.

▼ Rain forests receive large amounts of rain every year, providing the right environment for many species, including hornbills.

The Water Cycle

All types of ecosystems depend on Earth's great water cycle, or hydrologic cycle, for survival. Earth's water is used over and over again, but it is never used up. Almost all rainwater that falls to the planet's surface eventually finds its way back to the ocean. It may get there by flowing in rivers that empty into the sea, or it may slowly move through underground paths to the sea. Once in the ocean, the water is warmed by the Sun and eventually evaporates back into the atmosphere. In the atmosphere, the water vapor condenses into water droplets, which form clouds. The water then falls back to the ground as rain or other forms of precipitation.

Precipitation and Weather

The water cycle is a major driver of the world's weather. Water forms into various kinds of precipitation in the atmosphere, including rain, snow, sleet, and hail.

Rain forms when water vapor condenses around tiny particles, such as bits

▼ In Earth's water, or hydrologic, cycle, water is recycled from the atmosphere to surface bodies of water and underground streams, then to the ocean and back again to the atmosphere.

Water Cycle

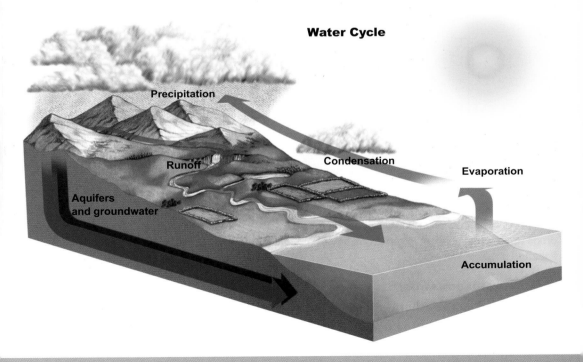

Precipitation

Runoff

Condensation

Evaporation

Aquifers and groundwater

Accumulation

2005, when Hurricane Katrina swept a path of destruction across Louisiana, Mississippi, and Alabama. The high winds, huge waves, and flooding led to the deaths of more than 1,700 people and left thousands homeless.

▲ Hurricane Claudette swirls over the Gulf coast of Texas in July 2003 in this photo taken by astronauts aboard the International Space Station.

Climate Change Over Time

Climate refers to the type of weather that occurs in a region over a long period. Earth is more than 4.5 billion years old. Its climate has been continuously changing. The average surface temperature changes over long periods of hundreds of years as does the average amount of precipitation.

Perhaps the most dramatic examples of climate change have been the recurring ice ages. These are long periods when temperatures drop and sheets of ice cover vast regions of land. There have been many ice ages in Earth's history, each one lasting approximately 100,000 years. In between these ice ages have been interglacial periods, when the ice sheets largely disappeared. These interglacial periods usually lasted between about 10,000 and 20,000 years. The most recent ice age ended about 11,500 years ago. What does that tell you Earth is in store for soon, perhaps within a few thousand years?

Glaciers, which are large masses of ice that move slowly over land, may have once occurred where Chicago and Berlin, Germany, are today. Now they are found mostly in Antarctica and Greenland and in high, cold mountain valleys. Glaciers form when year-round temperatures are so low that the snow that falls during winter does not melt or evaporate in spring. The snow builds up throughout the year and is compressed by its own weight until it forms ice.

Although it's hard to notice, glaciers actually move, usually less than 1 foot (30 cm) per day. The force of gravity tends to pull them downslope, and the melting and refreezing of ice crystals along the base of glaciers helps them slide along.

Glaciers shape the land by scooping out surface rock and gouging out depressions as the ice moves. As a glacier retreats, usually by melting, it leaves behind deposits of clay, sand, and rocks. You can see these deposits today as hills or ridges known as moraines.

Erosion

The force of flowing water is powerful enough to carve wide valleys and steep-sided canyons and to split mountains in half or reduce them to small hills. This process is known as erosion. The Grand Canyon in northern Arizona is an enormous desert gorge that was gradually cut out of the ground by the flowing waters of the Colorado River.

Terraces are another landform made by rivers. They are the remains of old floodplains formed as a winding river cuts down and sideways into its bed. As the river cuts deeper, it makes levels of plains, like long wide steps. Natural bridges form as rivers cut passages through rock.

▲ Double O Arch in Arches National Park in Utah has a large arch and, below that, a small arch, both of which were created by water erosion of sandstone.

Ocean waves cause erosion along seacoasts. Sea cliffs form where waves pound against a slope, undercutting it and leaving an overhanging top. Gravity may eventually cause the top to collapse. The pounding of waves can also form caves and arches along a shore. Sandbars form as wave action deposits sand from the shore in an area that builds up above the water's surface. Bays form when hard, resistant rock juts out as a headland after nearby, softer rock is worn away.

4 FRESHWATER AND SALT WATER

Water covers more than 70 percent of Earth's surface. Almost all of this water—97 percent—is salt water in the oceans and seas of the world. Only 3 percent is freshwater. Two thirds of that freshwater is locked up as ice in glaciers and in the ice caps around the North and South Poles. The remaining 1 percent of freshwater is found in rivers and lakes, underground, and in the atmosphere.

Rivers

Rivers are bodies of freshwater that flow in long channels. The two longest rivers, the Nile in Africa and the Amazon in South America, flow for about 4,000 miles (6,437 kilometers).

A river flows from its source to its mouth. The source, where the river's water originates, may be a melting snow-field, an underground spring, or an

Longest Rivers

River	Length, miles (km)	Location
Nile	4,160 (6,695)	Northeast Africa
Amazon	4,000 (6,437)	South America
Yangtze	3,915 (6,300)	China
Huang He	2,903 (4,672)	China
Congo	2,900 (4,667)	Africa
Mekong	2,600 (4,180)	Asia
Niger	2,600 (4,180)	Africa
Missouri	2,540 (4,090)	United States
Mississippi	2,340 (3,766)	United States
Volga	2,194 (3,531)	Russia

▲ The Nile, in Africa, is the longest river in the world.

overflowing lake. The mouth, where the river empties, may lead to a larger river, a lake, or the ocean. A delta, a wide area where the water slows and eroded soil builds up, often forms at the mouth of a river.

The region of land drained by a river system is called its drainage basin. This region can be vast. The Mississippi River drains 40 percent of the contiguous forty-eight states of the United States. The flat area at the sides of a riverbank that may be covered with water during floods is called the river's floodplain.

As a river flows, it may cross an area of hard rock that is resistant to erosion. A waterfall may form in such an area, as the water wears away at the softer, lower rock downstream from this hard spot. In some cases, the hard spot forms the edge of a tall, vertical cliff, over which a waterfall plunges. Some of the world's most dramatic, breathtaking waterfalls include Iguazu Falls in South America, Victoria Falls in Africa, and Niagara Falls in North America.

A wide variety of plants and animals live in or near rivers. The plants that grow on river floodplains must adapt to living in wet, submerged conditions for part of the year and dry conditions during other times. Among lowland plants

▲ Iguazu Falls is a group of about 275 waterfalls on the Iguazu River, some as high as 260 feet (80 m), that extend for 1.7 miles (2.7 km) along the border between Argentina and Brazil, in South America.

in North America are ash, elm, silver maple, and willow trees. Animals that live in rivers include insects (mostly in their larval, or immature, stages); crustaceans, such as crayfish and other shellfish; mollusks, such as clams; and many kinds of fish. River birds include kingfishers, which nest in tunnels in the walls of riverbanks, and such waterbirds as ducks and geese. Mammals that spend most of their time in rivers include otters and beavers.

Lakes

Lakes are bodies of water surrounded by land. Lakes may be fed by rivers, streams, mountain springs, or underground springs. Most lakes are filled by freshwater, but some contain salt water, like the water in the ocean. Saltwater lakes are called seas, such as the Aral, Caspian, and Dead Seas. Some lakes are very large. Lake Baikal, in Russia, is so large—reaching an area of 12,162 square miles (31,499 sq km) and a depth of 5,315 feet (1,620 m)—that it contains about one-fifth of all the freshwater in the world.

Many lakes you see today formed in regions that were once covered by glaciers, which gouged out hollows in the land and deposited ridges of rock and soil. Lakes eventually formed in these hollow spaces and uneven areas of land. Some lakes form in other ways. For example, an oxbow lake forms when a river changes course, leaving a separate curved channel behind.

The organisms in a lake are divided into three main types of habitat: open water, bottom, and emergent. In the open water, plankton (mostly microscopic animals and plantlike organisms) drift along, fish, turtles, ducks, and an occasional water snake swim. At the lake bottom can be found sponges, snails, clams, crayfish, worms, and insect larvae, such as mayfly and dragonfly nymphs. Bacteria at the bottom decompose the dead remains of lake organisms after they have sunk to the bottom. Plants such as cattails, sedges, and pickerelweeds are anchored at the shallow lake bottom near the shore but emerge out of the water.

The largest lakes, such as the Great Lakes, have a major influence on the weather of the surrounding area. Because of the great heat capacity of water, a large

How Lakes Form

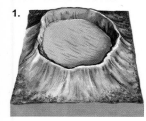 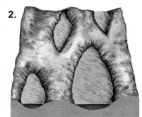  

▲ Different lakes form in different ways. Some lakes form in volcanic craters (1); others form in basins carved out of rock by glaciers (2); still others form when the buildup of sediment causes a river to change course, leaving a curved channel behind (3 and 4).

Thermocline

The warm and cold waters in large, deep lakes are separated by a layer called a thermocline. Warm water (the epilimnion) occurs above this layer. Then, the temperature of the water in the thermocline drops rapidly, and the water below (the hypolimnion) is cold. The thermocline normally keeps the warm water separated from the cold water. In spring and fall, however, the temperature of the upper layer becomes similar to that of the lower layer, and the two layers mix in what is known as an overturn. An overturn mixes nutrients from surface waters throughout the whole lake.

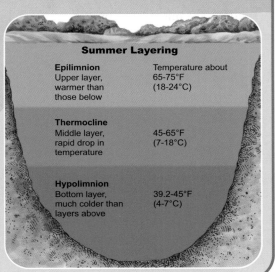

Summer Layering

Epilimnion
Upper layer, warmer than those below — Temperature about 65-75°F (18-24°C)

Thermocline
Middle layer, rapid drop in temperature — 45-65°F (7-18°C)

Hypolimnion
Bottom layer, much colder than layers above — 39.2-45°F (4-7°C)

Largest Lakes

Lake	Area in square miles (sq km)	Location
Caspian Sea*	143,250 (371,000)	Kazakhstan-Turkmenistan, Iran-Azerbaijan-Russia
Lake Superior	31,700 (82,103)	Canada-United States
Lake Victoria	26,828 (69,484)	Kenya-Tanzania-Uganda
Lake Huron	23,000 (59,600)	Canada-United States
Lake Michigan	22,300 (57,757)	United States
Lake Tanganyika	12,700 (32,893)	Burundi-Tanzania-Zambia-Congo
Lake Baikal	12,162 (31,499)	Russia
Aral Sea*	11,200 (28,680)	Kazakhstan-Uzbekistan
(* saltwater lake)		

lake is warmer than the surrounding land in winter and cooler in summer, so breezes blowing over the lake help warm the land in winter and cool it in summer.

Wetlands

Wetlands are areas of land where water remains near or above the surface of the ground for most of the year. Examples of freshwater wetlands include marshes, swamps, bogs, and fens.

Marshes are usually found in the shallow waters of lakes and streams. Swamps are usually found in wooded areas. Bogs and fens are wetlands that contain large amounts of peat, partially decayed plant material. The water of bogs has a high acid content, which prevents the growth of bacteria and slows the decomposition of dead organisms. People harvesting peat for fuel have found hundreds of almost perfectly preserved remains of people who died thousands of years ago in bogs in Denmark, Germany, Ireland, and the Netherlands.

Wetlands help control flooding because they can retain large amounts of water, kind of like a giant sponge. They are also the natural habitat for many plant and animal species, such as sedges, reeds, turtles, herons, cranes, alligators, and panthers.

▲ An alligator basks in the sun in the Everglades, a vast area of wetlands and other types of ecosystems in southern Florida.

Other Freshwater Environments

Most freshwater, other than that locked up in ice, occurs below Earth's surface as groundwater. As rain trickles into the ground, spaces between grains of sand and cracks and pores in rock become soaked up to a certain zone, known as the water table. Wells reach below the water table to the area of porous material, called an aquifer, to pump up water for human use.

Hot springs, or geysers, are places where hot rocks below the surface heat water, which then explodes out of the ground along with steam. Perhaps the most famous geyser is Old Faithful, in Yellowstone National Park, which has erupted every 30 to 120 minutes since at least the early 1900s.

Brackish waters

Some bodies of water have some freshwater and some salt water—that is, they are brackish, or slightly salty.

Salt marshes are brackish bodies of water along coasts where freshwater flows into the ocean, such as at the mouth of a river. Mangrove swamps are brackish forests along many tropical shores. Mangrove trees help protect coastal areas from the full force of waves generated by storms.

Some lakes are brackish environments. For example, Lake Pontchartrain is a brackish lake in southeastern Louisiana, near New Orleans.

The Ocean

The global ocean covers most of Earth's surface, which is why our planet appears mostly blue as seen from space. Ocean water contains about 3.5 percent salt, which is mostly sodium chloride (NaCl), the same type of salt used on food.

The continents divide the global ocean into three major parts. The largest part is the Pacific Ocean, with North and South America on the east and Asia and Australia on the west. It covers about one-third of Earth's surface. The two other major parts are the Atlantic Ocean, with Europe and Africa on the east and North and South America on the west, and the Indian Ocean, between Australia and Indonesia on the east and Africa on the west.

The Arctic Ocean, located north of North America, Europe, and Asia, is often considered part of the Atlantic Ocean. The Antarctic, or Southern, Ocean, which surrounds Antarctica, is usually considered the most southern parts of the Pacific, the Atlantic, and the Indian Oceans.

Many rather small parts of the global ocean, known as seas, branch from the main parts of the ocean adjoining the continents throughout the world. Among the largest of these seas are the Bering Sea, Caribbean Sea, Mediterranean Sea, and North Sea.

The Ocean Floor

Scientists and explorers have discovered that the bottom of the ocean is an exciting, alien place. A chain of mountains, made up of mid-ocean ridges, stretches across the bottom of the main basins of the global ocean for at least 37,000 miles (60,000 km). These are places where giant tectonic plates—which are several shifting rocky slabs that make up Earth's crust—move apart, allowing volcanic magma, which is hot, liquefied rock, to rise from below the seafloor. Deep ocean trenches form at sites where one plate is forced downward as it butts up against another.

At several places along the mid-ocean ridges, scientists have discovered hydrothermal vents, places where mineral-rich water flows from the seafloor at temperatures up to 840°F (450°C).

▼ Marine scientists prepare the *Pisces V* submersible for exploration near the Loihi Seamount, an underwater volcano in the Hawaiian Islands.

Studying the Seafloor

Scientists use a number of methods to study the seafloor. Sonar is a method in which sound waves generated by special devices on ships are used to analyze features on the seafloor. The reflection of the sound waves, like echoes, gives the researchers information about the features at the bottom of the sea. Submersibles are vehicles that can carry human crews to the ocean floor. Remotely controlled submersibles can carry video cameras that show crews on surface ships what the seafloor looks like.

Diverse communities of unusual animals live around hydrothermal vents, including giant clams and tubeworms. Unlike almost all other animal communities on Earth, animals at hydrothermal vents live in an ecosystem without sunlight and photosynthesis. Instead of having plants create food through photosynthesis for the rest of the community, organisms at the deep, dark hydrothermal vents rely on microorganisms to produce food from minerals in the vent waters—a process called chemosynthesis.

Oceans and Seas

Ocean/Sea	Area, in million square miles (million sq km)
Pacific Ocean	64.0 (165.7)
Atlantic Ocean	31.8 (82.4)
Indian Ocean	28.3 (73.4)
Arctic Ocean	5.4 (14.1)
Gulf of Mexico/ Caribbean Sea	1.7 (4.3)
South China Sea	1.3 (3.4)
Mediterranean Sea	1.1 (3.0)
Black Sea	0.9 (2.3)
Bering Sea	0.6 (1.6)
Sea of Okhotsk	0.5 (1.2)
East China Sea	0.5 (1.2)
Hudson Bay	0.3 (0.8)

Life in the Ocean

Scientists divide life in the ocean into three general groups, based on the parts of the sea where the organisms live: plankton, nekton, and benthos.

The plankton group consists of tiny plantlike organisms (phytoplankton) and tiny animals (zooplankton) that drift with the ocean currents. Although they are small, these organisms are enormously important. The phytoplankton form the base of the food chain, producing food and energy for other life through photosynthesis. Zooplankton, such as the shrimplike krill, are major food sources for larger animals, including fish, birds, seals, squid, and whales.

The nekton are animals that swim freely, mostly near the sea surface. Fish, squid, seals, walruses, and whales are all parts of the nekton.

The benthos group consists of organisms that live on or near the ocean floor. There are many kinds of bizarre fish that live in these murky depths, including some that glow in the dark through a process called bioluminescence, in which light is produced through chemical reactions rather than heat. Sponges, starfish, sea urchins, marine worms, clams, and lobsters are other animals that are common in the benthic zone.

Weather Control

The ocean helps control the weather, partly because of its enormous heat capacity. Just like a giant lake, an ocean is warmer in winter and cooler in summer than the nearby land, so breezes blowing across the sea have a moderating effect on coastal weather conditions.

In addition, surface currents carry warm water from tropical areas to temperate areas, warming the atmosphere over temperate lands. That is why the Gulf Stream, flowing from the Gulf of Mexico to the northern Atlantic Ocean, helps keep Great Britain, Ireland, and most of western Europe warmer than they would be otherwise.

▼ The oceans of the world include numerous surface currents that flow near the coasts of the continents.

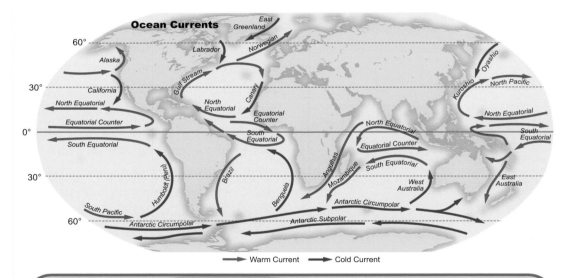

Ocean Currents

Warm Current   Cold Current

Lost City

A team of explorers led by Deborah Kelley, a geologist at the University of Washington in Seattle, discovered an unusual hydrothermal vent community along the Mid-Atlantic Ridge in 2000. Dubbed the "Lost City," the vent chimneys, structures made of minerals, are the tallest ever seen—up to 180 feet (55 m) high—and are made of light-colored calcium carbonate and silica compounds, rather than the dark iron and sulfur known from previously discovered vents. The microbes at the Lost City live in water that is nearly as caustic as drain opener.

5 WATER IN THE SOLAR SYSTEM

Earth is the only planet in our solar system—or the rest of the universe—known to have liquid water on its surface. Scientists are searching for evidence of past or present water on other planets and moons in our solar system, as well as around other stars.

Comets

Orbiting the Sun at the distant edges of our solar system are many thousands of small bodies containing water ice. The bodies, known as comets, are sometimes called "dirty snowballs" because they consist of a mix of ice, rock, and dust particles. Scientists believe that comets are "leftover" objects from the dust, gas, ice, and rocks that formed our solar system more than 4.5 billion years ago.

There are two main zones in which comets normally are located—the Kuiper belt, which lies beyond the orbit of Neptune, and the Oort cloud, far beyond the orbit of Pluto. The passing of a star nearby may generate gravitational forces that nudge a comet out of either of these zones and onto a path toward the inner solar system.

Comets can best be seen from Earth when the Sun's warmth causes material from a comet's nucleus (solid core) to vaporize, resulting in the formation of a gassy atmosphere, called a coma, around the nucleus. The solar wind, a stream of electrically charged particles flowing from the Sun, causes some gas, dust, and ions (electrically charged atoms) that come off the comet to stretch out into one or two long tails.

If a comet gets too close to the Sun or planets, gravity may pull it into a crash encounter. That is why comets have sometimes crashed into Earth. In fact, some scientists believe that comets may have been the source of much of the water that early Earth came to have.

Mars

Of all eight planets in our solar system, one has captured the public's imagination as the most likely place where liquid water—and life—might be found. That planet is Mars, which orbits the Sun one and one-half times farther away than Earth.

Scientists have determined that Mars has quite a lot of water, although most of this water is frozen as ice—along with carbon dioxide ice—at the planet's poles. On Mars, frozen water exists as permafrost below the surface. Scientists have estimated that if all the water ice on Mars melted, it would cover the red planet's surface with a global ocean about 98 feet (30 m) deep. Mars is too cold today for liquid water to remain on its surface.

One reason Mars is so cold is that it has a very thin atmosphere—much too thin to trap the Sun's heat that is radiated from the planet's surface. By contrast, Earth has a thick atmosphere, which acts

▼ A photograph of the surface of Mars taken by the *Mars Global Surveyor* spacecraft in 2000 shows what appear to be dried gullies formed by liquid water. Some scientists believe that seepage or runoff of water might have formed these features within the past few years.

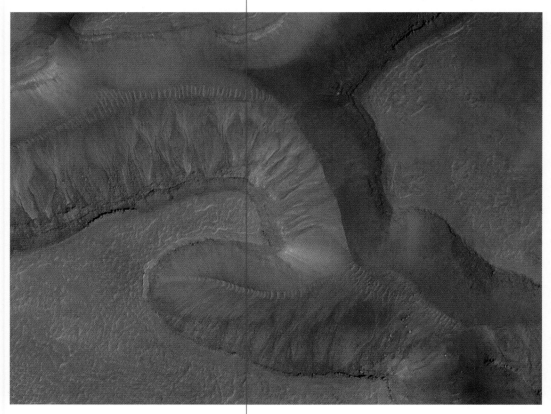

as an invisible blanket to keep heat near the surface—a process known as the "greenhouse effect." Thin clouds of frozen carbon dioxide and water often form in the atmosphere of Mars. Frosts, mists, and fogs of water ice also often form on Mars.

Evidence indicates that, perhaps 3 to 4 billion years ago, Mars had a thicker atmosphere and was much warmer than it is today—warm enough for water to flow on its surface. Orbiting spacecraft have photographed long, winding channels on Mars, channels that resemble dried riverbeds.

Spacecraft have also photographed gullies in the walls of craters on Mars. Scientists say these gullies could have formed within the past few million years, or even as soon as the past few years, when sudden bursts of water quickly leaked from below the ground. The low temperatures and low atmospheric pressure on Mars would not have allowed water to stay liquid for long, however. So the water would have rapidly frozen and then changed from a solid to a gas, a process known as sublimation.

The *2001 Mars Odyssey* spacecraft used an instrument called a gamma ray spectrometer to discover that the upper 3 feet (1 m) of Martian soil contains large amounts of water ice. Each kind of chemical element gives off a special type of high-energy ray. The gamma ray spectrometer on *Mars Odyssey* detected rays indicating that the element hydrogen was below the surface. The project's scientists interpreted this hydrogen as being from water ice. Scientists believe that Mars may also have deep reservoirs of liquid water, kept warm by the internal heat of the planet.

In 2004, while exploring a region of Mars called Meridiani Planum, the *Spirit* and *Opportunity* robotic rovers detected chemical compounds that usually form in bodies of salt water. Scientists think that Meridiani Planum may have once had a salty lake or sea.

Exobiology

Exobiology is the branch of biology that specializes in the search for life elsewhere in the universe. Exobiologists use space probes with instruments that can perform chemical analyses, looking for evidence of water or organic compounds (the chemicals that are produced by plant and animal activities). Some exobiologists use radio telescopes to study radio signals from space, looking for patterns that suggest that the signals might have been produced by intelligent civilizations.

Life on Mars?

Could there be life on Mars today? Life on the surface is highly unlikely for two reasons. There is no liquid water, which all known life needs, and the atmosphere is too thin to block the harmful ultraviolet rays from the Sun, which would be lethal to any surface life. Still, scientists believe it might be possible for some kinds of life to exist in watery environments below the surface. These organisms might be similar to so-called extremophile microbes that have been found deep below the surface of Earth.

Europa

Another space object that could possibly have life is Europa. It is one of the four large moons that orbit Jupiter, the fifth planet from the Sun.

Europa, which is slightly smaller than Earth's moon, has a surface covered with ice that may be between 50 and 100 miles (80 and 160 km) thick. Deep cracks run through the ice, forming huge icy chunks that shift in position, much as Earth's icebergs do.

Galileo Visits Jupiter

The *Galileo* spacecraft, the first craft to orbit Jupiter, studied the giant planet and its moons from 1995 to 2003. *Galileo* found strong evidence that an ocean of water or soft ice lies beneath Europa's surface. *Galileo* also released a small probe into the atmosphere of Jupiter. The probe found less water vapor in Jupiter's clouds than was expected.

This photo collage shows Jupiter *(upper right)* and its four largest moons—*(from upper left to lower right)* Io, Europa, Ganymede, and Callisto. Scientists believe that Europa is likely to have an ocean of liquid water beneath its icy surface.

Scientists have concluded that a deep, dark ocean of liquid water might exist below Europa's thick icy layer. This conclusion is based on the way the ice chunks change position, like drifting ice on Earth's ocean. In addition, dark brownish material can be seen in the ice cracks. This material looks like dark contaminants erupting from either subsurface water or slushy ice.

How could liquid water exist on frozen Europa? Internal heat on Europa is generated by the gravitational forces of Jupiter and the other moons of Jupiter in a process called tidal flexing. In this process, the different gravitational forces pull at Europa's interior in different directions, causing geological stresses that result in friction and heating.

If Europa does have an ocean below its ice, it is possible that some kind of life-forms exist in this dark alien sea. American and European scientists have proposed landing a spacecraft on Europa to melt through the ice and study the ocean believed to exist on the moon.

Extrasolar Planets

In the 1990s, astronomers began to discover planets around other stars. By 2006, they had found more than 160 such extrasolar worlds, and they continue to find more.

How do scientists discover such distant planets? In one method, called the radial velocity method, tiny "wobbles" in the movement of a star can be detected. These wobbles indicate that the gravity of an orbiting planet is tugging at the star. In another method, called the transit method, the brightness of a star dims slightly as a planet passes in front of it. The amount of dimming provides clues as to the planet's size, the density of its atmosphere, and its orbital period.

Most of the extrasolar planets that have been found are not like Earth. They are giants even larger than Jupiter. Some of these planets may have clouds of water ice in their atmospheres, much as Jupiter has been shown to have.

Such planets are too small to spot with the limited technology available to astronomers today. However, scientists are making progress. In 2004, the first extrasolar planets the size of Neptune and Uranus, which are smaller than Jupiter but still much larger than Earth, were detected. Scientists are confident that it is only a matter of time until they detect the first Earthlike planets that are capable of having amounts of liquid water on their surfaces.

6 WATER – A VITAL RESOURCE

Water has been perhaps the most important factor in the development of human civilizations. It has always been used for growing food, bathing, cooking, cleaning, carrying away wastes, and producing power. Rivers and oceans have always been avenues for transportation, trade, and exploration. Fish, shellfish, and other animals that live in water have always been important foods for people. Today, however, a number of problems threaten the continued easy access to water supplies that people have long taken for granted.

Role of Water in Human Civilizations

For thousands of years, civilizations around the world have arisen where water supplies were plentiful and where food could be obtained from bodies of water. These civilizations include ancient Mesopotamia by the Tigris and Euphrates Rivers, in modern Iraq; Egypt by the Nile River; and Greece and Rome by the Mediterranean Sea. Great eastern civilizations arose along rivers in India

Collapse of Sumer

Many historians believe that the ancient Sumerian civilization of Mesopotamia (modern Iraq) collapsed because of poor irrigation practices, which resulted in too much salt and waterlogged soil that destroyed the farmland.

▼ The Pont du Gard aqueduct was constructed by the Romans in about 19 B.C. to carry water where it was needed. The structure crosses the Gard River near Nimes, France.

and China. In the Americas, areas along the Mississippi and Amazon Rivers, the Gulf of Mexico coast, and the Atlantic and Pacific Oceans were the sites of many original native settlements.

Today, water is important for many uses beyond those of ancient peoples. Hydroelectric power stations use the energy of falling water from waterfalls or river dams to produce electricity. Industries use water as a raw material in canned foods, pharmaceuticals, paints, and other products, as well as for cooling and cleaning purposes. Medicines are obtained from marine life, such as a drug to prevent blood clotting that is obtained from red algae. People also use water for a wide range of recreational activities, such as swimming, boating, and fishing.

▲ The Hoover Dam hydroelectric power plant, in the Black Canyon of the Colorado River on the Arizona-Nevada border, provides electric power for much of the Pacific Southwest region. Transmission towers *(inset)* help distribute the electricity.

Hydroelectricity

Hydroelectric facilities use the power of water in rivers or waterfalls to produce electrical energy. One cubic foot (0.028 cubic meter) of water weighs about 62 pounds (28 kilograms), so gravity creates a pressure of 6,240 pounds (2,830 kg) per square foot at the base of a waterfall 100 feet (30.5 m) tall. Hydroelectric power plants can convert such large amounts of pressure into electrical power.

Water Pollution

Water pollution has long been a problem in many rivers, lakes, groundwater supplies, and parts of the ocean. These bodies of water may be contaminated with human and animal wastes, toxic industrial chemicals, harmful agricultural pesticides and fertilizers, and disease-causing bacteria and viruses.

Pollutants cause problems in several ways. For example, when phosphorus-

and nitrogen-based fertilizers from farms are washed into lakes or other bodies of water, they act as nutrients for the algae that live in the water. The populations of these plantlike organisms multiply. Then, after the algae die and settle at the bottom of the body of water, they are decomposed by bacteria. Oxygen from the water is used up by the billions of bacteria performing decomposition. As the oxygen level in the water falls, fish and other animals dependent on these oxygen supplies die. This process is called eutrophication.

Acid rain is rain or other precipitation that is polluted with sulfuric acid or nitric acid, corrosive chemical compounds that form from other compounds

▼ A carved figure on the side of a church in England shows erosion caused by acid rain.

released by automobiles, factories, and power plants. Acid rain can wear away parts of buildings, contaminate soil, and cause damage to natural environments, such as lakes, rivers, and forests.

Reducing Water Pollution

Water pollution is less of a problem today than it was during the mid- to late-twentieth century—thanks to the efforts of concerned citizens who helped get the government to pass legislation controlling pollution. Two landmark antipollution laws enacted by the U.S. government were the Clean Water Act of 1971 and the Safe Drinking Water Act of 1974.

The Clean Water Act gave the U.S. Environmental Protection Agency (EPA) the power to establish regulations and programs to reduce the discharge of pollutants into waterways. The Safe Drinking Water Act authorized the EPA to set standards to reduce harmful bacteria, chemicals, and metallic compounds in public water systems.

Progress in cleaning up water pollution is evident in many bodies of water. The Cuyahoga River, in northern Ohio, was formerly so polluted with industrial chemicals, oils, and floating debris that it actually caught fire several times between the 1930s and 1960s. Finally, actions were taken to address the river's sources of pollution, including reducing chemical discharges by industries along the river. Today, the water quality of the Cuyahoga River is dramatically improved, and recreational parks, protected natural areas, and entertainment facilities line the riverbank.

Most of the Great Lakes were once heavily polluted with industrial chemicals and agricultural wastes. Since the United States and Canada signed an agreement in 1972 to reduce this pollution, the water quality of all the lakes has greatly improved. Still, some toxic chemicals remain in the lakes, contaminating certain kinds of fish.

Sources of Water Pollution

- Agricultural fertilizers and pesticides
- Animal wastes from feed lots
- Burning of coal, oil, and other fossil fuels by factories and power plants
- Coal-fired boilers, municipal incinerators, and smelters
- Emissions from automobiles, trucks, and other motor vehicles
- Human sewage
- Industrial chemical wastes

▼ Water pollution comes from many sources, including wastes from farms, untreated human sewage, and rainwater containing air pollutants. Some of these pollutants reduce the water's oxygen content, killing fish.

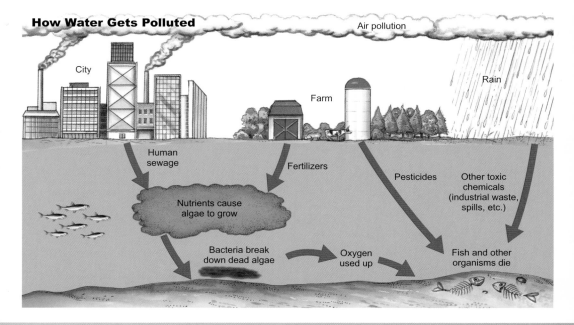

How Water Gets Polluted

Air pollution

City

Farm

Rain

Human sewage

Fertilizers

Pesticides

Other toxic chemicals (industrial waste, spills, etc.)

Nutrients cause algae to grow

Bacteria break down dead algae

Oxygen used up

Fish and other organisms die

City Water Treatment

Most cities obtain their water supplies from rivers, lakes, or groundwater. Before this water is delivered to the residents of a city, it goes through a number of chemical and physical processes to remove harmful bacteria, chemical compounds, minerals, and other impurities, and to eliminate bad tastes and odors. In addition, many cities add fluoride to their water supplies to help reduce tooth decay.

Water treatment processes are not designed to remove all contaminants from water supplies. Rather, these processes keep the contaminants below levels that would be harmful to human health. The governments of many cities mail water quality reports to the city residents so that they can see the levels of contaminants found in their water supplies.

Overfishing

Large fleets of modern fishing boats are like floating factories, catching and processing fish in enormous quantities that were unheard of just decades ago. Overfishing has become a major threat to the biodiversity of the oceans. The stocks of many types of fish, including cod and haddock, have declined dramatically.

The decline in fish stocks has had a negative impact on the fishing industry, which is increasingly finding it difficult to catch certain kinds of fish in the ocean. As a result, many nations have taken action to promote fish conservation. Many countries have also adopted zones along their coasts in which they claim authority over all fishing and ownership of all fish and other natural resources.

Global Warming

Scientists have documented a gradual rise in Earth's average surface temperature since the late 1800s. Most scientists believe that this warming trend, known as global warming, is being caused mainly by the burning of fossil fuels—coal, oil, and natural gas—that release carbon dioxide gas into the atmosphere. A so-called greenhouse gas, carbon dioxide, allows sunlight to enter the atmosphere but then traps some of the infrared (heat) rays radiated by Earth's surface and reflects them back toward Earth.

The carbon dioxide produced through human activities is enhancing Earth's natural greenhouse effect. How this will ultimately affect Earth's climate and water cycle is open to dispute. Many scientists believe that continued warming could cause glaciers and ice sheets to melt, raising sea levels dramatically and flooding many coastal regions. Many experts believe that the temperature changes will significantly alter rainfall patterns, resulting in increased flooding in some regions and increased drought in other areas. These scientists point to evidence that some glaciers on mountaintops in the Andes, the European Alps, and elsewhere, along with sea ice around the Antarctic Peninsula, are shrinking.

Other scientists, however, point out that Earth's climate is extremely complex and cannot be easily understood or predicted using the computer models, on which most global warming predictions are based. In addition, some scientists believe that the current warming is due more to Earth's natural cycle of warming and cooling than to the burning of fossil fuels.

▼ The greenhouse effect is caused by greenhouse gases, such as carbon dioxide, methane, and water vapor, which allow sunlight to enter the atmosphere but trap some of the infrared (heat) rays from Earth's surface. This process is similar to the way that windows in a greenhouse trap the heat that plants need to grow.

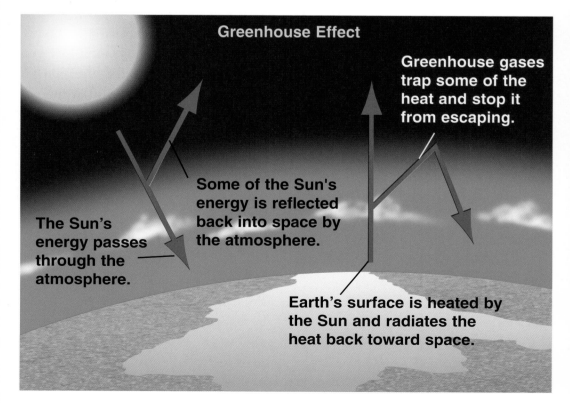

Greenhouse Effect

Greenhouse gases trap some of the heat and stop it from escaping.

Some of the Sun's energy is reflected back into space by the atmosphere.

The Sun's energy passes through the atmosphere.

Earth's surface is heated by the Sun and radiates the heat back toward space.

Despite the scientific disputes, many nations have taken steps to restrict industrial emissions of carbon dioxide to help reduce any possible effects from global warming. The Kyoto Protocol, signed by most of the world's countries, requires industrialized nations to restrict emissions of greenhouse gases from 2008 through 2012. Although the United States rejected the Kyoto Protocol in 2001, U.S. officials have promised to help limit greenhouse gas emissions by requiring automakers to make more fuel-efficient cars.

Water Shortages

As the human population grows, the demand for water is increasing. Many parts of the world today face severe water shortages. Millions of people in Africa, Asia, and South America have no running water and no access to safe drinking water. The United Nations warned in 2003 that more than half of humanity could be living with serious water shortages by 2050.

The problem, however, is not a lack of water. Because of the continual recycling of water in the water cycle, there is as much water on Earth today as there ever was. The real problem is that supplies of water are often mismanaged. In many countries, governments have not invested enough resources in water storage facilities, water treatment plants, or water distribution services.

Many experts warn that unless today's water shortages are addressed in ways that are fair to all people, not only will millions of people die, but wars are likely to erupt over access to water in places such as the Middle East. The global water shortage may be the most important issue facing humanity in the early 2000s.

Water Conservation

Human history has always revolved around water, and water plays vital roles in all areas of science, including biology, ecology, and geology. Yet, in the United States and many other industrial nations, water is cheap. As a result, many people take water for granted, using it carelessly and wasting it. However, if we hope to prevent a future crisis concerning water, we need to use this important resource more wisely.

Many cities try to conserve water by rationing its use during hot, dry spells. Some industries recycle water in circulating cooling systems. Some farmers try to prevent water loss by planting trees and other vegetation with extensive roots to slow water runoff through the soil. Desalination facilities use technological processes to remove salt from seawater so that it can be used for drinking, agriculture, and other purposes.

These are all important means of water conservation. What can you do to help? You can use water more efficiently and reduce your consumption of water by changing certain behaviors in your home and yard. Some of these behavioral changes are listed in the table on this page.

As you think about ways to save water, remember how important water is to everything people do and to the survival of all plant and animal life. Living with water and taking care not to waste it is all part of living on Earth, the water world.

Amount of Water It Takes to Perform Various Activities

Activity	Amount of water, gallons (liters)	
Produce 1 ton (0.9 metric ton) of paper	38,000	(144,000)
Grow enough wheat to bake a loaf of bread	115	(435)
Use washing machine	40	(152)
Take a bath	30	(114)
Wash dishes	15	(57)
Flush toilet	7	(26)
Spend one minute in shower	5	(19)

How You Can Conserve Water
- Run the dishwasher only when full.
- If washing dishes by hand, fill the sink with water; do not let the water run.
- Turn off the faucet while brushing your teeth.
- Take short showers, and turn off the water while soaping.
- Use low-flow showerheads.
- Use toilets only to carry away human wastes.
- Adjust water levels on washing machine to match size of loads.
- Water lawn only in the early morning or late evening, to reduce evaporation.
- Allow grass to grow taller to promote water retention in soil.
- When washing cars, turn off the hose between rinses.

GLOSSARY

adaptation Characteristic of an organism that makes it better able to survive and reproduce in its environment

adhesive force Force that causes two unlike substances to stick together because of the attraction between molecules and atoms

amino acid Any of twenty types of organic acids that make up the proteins in living organisms

antibody Protein substance made in the blood or tissues that destroys or weakens bacteria or the poisons they produce

aquifer An area of earth or porous rock below ground that contains water

axis Imaginary line through the North and South Poles around which a planet or any other body rotates

biodiversity Variety that exists among different species of plants, animals, and other organisms

bioluminescence Emission of light resulting from biological or chemical processes

chemical bond Strong attraction between two or more atoms due to the sharing or transfer of electrons between bonded atoms

climate Type of weather that occurs in a region over a long period

cohesive force Force that holds a material together because of the attraction between molecules and atoms in the material

computer model Electronic representation of objects or ideas that respond to changing factors, based on sets of mathematical equations

condensation Changing of a gas or vapor into a liquid by cooling

electron Subatomic particle carrying one unit of negative electricity

equator Imaginary circle around Earth halfway between the North and South Poles

eutrophication Accumulation of nutrients in lakes and other bodies of water, causing rapid growth of algae and depletion of oxygen in the water

evaporation The process by which a liquid is changed into a gas (or vapor)

full moon The Moon seen as a whole circle; happens when Earth is directly between the Sun and the Moon

hormone Substance formed in endocrine glands that enters the bloodstream and affects or controls the activity of cells, tissues, or organs

hydrogen bond Bond that links one water molecule to another because the positive electrical charge at one end of a water molecule attracts the negative charge at one end of another water molecule

infrared Refers to electromagnetic rays responsible for the heat from sunlight, incandescent lamps, and other sources

kinetic energy Energy an object has because it is in motion

mid-ocean ridge Any of the large ridges running through the middle of the Atlantic Ocean and across the Pacific Ocean

moraine Mass or ridge of rocks, dirt, and other debris deposited by a glacier as the glacier melts

neutron Subatomic particle that is electrically neutral and has about the same mass as a proton

new moon The Moon when the side facing the Earth appears dark; it happens when the Moon is directly between Earth and the Sun

permafrost Layer of permanently frozen soil found near the surface in arctic regions

proton Subatomic particle carrying one unit of positive electricity

sublimation Process in which a solid turns into vapor

tectonic plates About thirty large, rigid pieces of Earth's crust that drift about above a hot, flowing layer of rock

thermocline Layer in a large body of water in which the temperature changes abruptly, separating warm waters above from cool waters below

tide Rise and fall of the ocean caused by the gravitational attraction of the Moon and Sun

transpiration Giving off of water by the leaves of a plant

water table Level below which the ground is saturated with water

FURTHER INFORMATION

Books
Earle, Sylvia A. *National Geographic Atlas of the Ocean*. Washington, DC: National Geographic Society, 2001.

Hooper, Meredith Jean and Chris Coady. *The Drop in My Drink: The Story of Water on Our Planet*. New York: Viking Juvenile, 1998.

Lawlor, Elizabeth P. and Pat Archer. *Discover Nature in Water & Wetlands: Things to Know and Things to Do* (Discover Nature series). Mechanicsburg, PA: Stackpole Books, 2000.

Martin, Patricia A. Fink. *Rivers and Streams*. New York: Franklin Watts, 1999.

Outwater, Alice B. *Water: A Natural History*. New York: Basic Books, 1997.

Villiers, Marq de. *Water: The Fate of Our Most Precious Resource*. Boston: Mariner Books, 2001.

Web Sites
Animal Planet—Animals A to Zoo—Water Life
animal.discovery.com/guides/atoz/water.html

BBC News—World Water Crisis
news.bbc.co.uk/hi/english/static/in_depth/world/2000/world_water_crisis/default.stm

U.S. Environmental Protection Agency—Water
www.epa.gov/water

U.S. Geological Survey—Water Science for Schools
ga.water.usgs.gov/edu

U.S. National Oceanic and Atmospheric Administration—Ocean Explorer
www.oceanexplorer.noaa.gov

DVDs
Glaciers: Alaska's Rivers of Ice. DVD International, 2003.

IMAX Presents: *Ocean Oasis—Two Worlds, One Paradise*. Magic Play, 2001.

Jean-Michel Cousteau's Ocean Adventures. PBS Paramount, 2006.

Nova—Mars, Dead or Alive. WGBH Boston, 2004.

INDEX